W9-ATM-693

STAFFORD CLIFF

1000
GARDEN
IDEAS

ARTISAN

NEW YORK

Plants aren't the only thing that you need to think about when you are creating a garden. In fact—with so many garden centers, plant catalogs, and farmers' markets around—plants are now one of the easiest things to find. But what about all the other decisions you need to make? The paths, the paving, the pots, the fencing, and the gate? Would you like a bench and a table, a water feature, a birdhouse, or a bridge? What should they look like? How would they fit into the rest of your garden plan? And how can you use them creatively and effectively? Whatever it is you may want to do, someone has likely done it before, and if you've ever been on a local garden tour or visited a famous garden or country estate, you will have realized that this is the best way to pick up good ideas—if only you could store them away until you need them; if only you could find so many that you'd have lots of choices for every gardening problem you're ever likely to need to solve; if only you could gather them all into an album of garden ideas. Now you don't need to. For the first time, they're all here—forty years of garden visits, all carried out with a designer's eye, to spot the cleverest solutions, the best answers, the most original choices, and to present them all in the most comprehensive collection of garden ideas you could ever find.

GATES

Walk up and down your street, explore your neighborhood, your town. Why are all the front gates so boring? A front gate is an opportunity to show how individual we are, how creative, how inventive. Perhaps, because they tend to be made from either wood or metal, they perish or rust away more quickly than other garden elements, like walls and paths. If your gate is at the back of the house, or in a side wall, it will be a different size and shape than one at the front. Sometimes, when we move in, they're missing altogether, and we're at a loss to know what design to choose or, indeed, if we need one at all. On the other hand, in a street where all the houses are built in the same style or are of the same period, there may be a perception that the gate belongs more to the façade of the building than to the plantings or the personality of the owner. Certainly there are streets in London or Paris or Toronto or Boston where all the fences and gates are part of the urban architecture and you cannot change even the color. For the rest, look around for something that suits you, your home, and the way you live. Think of it as a chance to add a little design flourish that would be inappropriate on a larger scale—like a stamp on a letter.

WALLS & FENCES

The best frame for a garden is a fence or wall. In choosing your frame, you need to ask yourself these three simple questions: Do you want to see the fence or cover it up with some kind of climbing plant? Do you want to see through it or block out what is beyond it? Finally, do you want to keep something out or keep something in? Most of us need a fence of some kind, but not one so high that it blocks out the light and annoys our neighbors. If you need only to demarcate the margins of your domain, then a simple post and rail job will do. But a fence or wall can do much more. It serves as a defining factor—finishing off a space and providing an element of protection and a vertical surface with which to be creative. And creativity is the key, since there is now a huge supply of possibilities, from pickets, mellow old brick, and stone, to concrete, ribbed and perforated metal, corrugated iron, and glass block. Some are permanent; some are more temporary. Some harmonize with the style of the house; others create a contrast. Some let light through; some retain heat and block the wind. Some you can assemble yourself, buying the components and taking them home in a car; some require a carpenter, a mason, or a building contractor; and for some you might need a salvage yard.

TILES, PATHS &
PAVING

EDGING

If we imagine a garden as a poem or a short story, edging is the punctuation, and a fence is a period. Edgings are vital to the flow of the planting, joining one phrase to another, coordinating a number of different or similar ideas, and knitting the picture together. Yet if they are so important, why are edgings so often overlooked or uninspired? Think of the horizontal surfaces in a garden as a number of personalities meeting each other. Some, like flowers and low hedges, get on well together, whereas others—hard and soft characters, like lawn and path—are best kept apart. How the edging works will depend on the style of your garden. If it's rustic, your solution will be found in the countryside—rocks, miniature fences, or, perhaps, an old log; if it's contemporary, your answers are more likely to come from urban architecture and the use of modern materials—concrete, steel, slate, brick, acrylic, or even glass. Finally, if you're feeling up to the challenge, consider recycling something. Blue bottles sunk upside down into the earth, partially embedded broken terra-cotta pots or even old dinner plates; for straight paths, old railroad ties are widely available. Failing all else, there are the products that are made for the job: molded tiles, latticed willow fences, or reproductions of antique French iron railings.

STEPS

More than perhaps any other element in the garden, steps are the most fascinating, with the most possibilities. They take us from one level to another, they change our perspective of the space, and they present endless opportunities. From the bottom, we see one aspect—the risers, or upright bits; from the top, we see the treads; and in midflight we see both. So, why are steps so often ignored, built of dull gray concrete or drab stone? Can't we be more creative? Perhaps we just need inspiration. Even steps that come with the property are not too difficult to replace. Adding different levels to a garden can be a costly and daunting prospect; and consequently, steps are usually limited to only two or three wide treads. Many of the most fascinating gardens are hilly, with steps that wind up out of sight, turn a corner, or stop and start seemingly at will. Steps also afford all sorts of areas for plantings; they need a beginning and an end; and they need edges—all providing a chance to embellish. At the same time, many homes are built on hills, or have steps leading to the entrance. Why should they be any less important a chance for self-expression than the gate, the path, or, indeed, the front door?

POTS

Pots are the most flexible of all the elements in the garden. You can move them around until you find the best position, you can bring them forward when the plants they contain are in flower, and you can, of course, change the plants in them as often as you like. You can—and I hope you will—have lots of pots in lots of shapes and sizes, like colorful ties to dress up the same dark suit. But pots are not just for plants; they can contain water, pebbles, twigs, or even fish. They are available in an abundance of different materials with plain or matte finishes, glazed in rich colors or embellished with a multitude of designs. More elaborate containers look best with modest sculptural contents, whereas a showy cascading plant might need a simpler pot. Finally, there are the urns, the "grandes dames" of pots, which have a design heritage that can be traced back to the Renaissance. Aloof on a plinth, they are objects in their own right. Though pots are currently the most fashionable design accessory in the garden, don't be limited by what you see in the garden center. Search out salvage yards or even find a local potter and commission him or her to create your own shape, or copy one of the examples that follow.

CHAIRS, SEATS & BENCHES

A bench is not only a place to sit. Whether it's made from wood or concrete, stone or metal, a bench (or a seat) also functions like a piece of sculpture—an object that adds to the character of your garden and a relief from the softness of the flowers and foliage. The size, the form, and the design of the piece—and where you place it—are as important as what it's like to sit on. It should be comfortable, but it should also look comfortable—as well as being in keeping with the size and style of your garden: classical and grand, modern and architectural, or twiggy and rustic. Some benches are meant to stay out all year round, growing more attractive as they slowly weather, acquiring a patina of moss or rust. Others are too fragile and are designed to be folded up and put away after the summer. Some of the best have tailor-made or improvised cushions that appear each morning, and some—perhaps close to the house—form part of a cluster of furniture that provides a spot for lunches or candlelit summer dinners. But on its own, a bench is also a marker. It says that over here, there is a nice viewpoint, the best vista, the most sheltered or sunny aspect or a shady, cool retreat. It signals to everyone that if you sit for a while, you won't be disappointed.

STATUES
& OTHER OBJECTS

The tradition of having statues dotted around the garden dates back to the Italian gardens of the sixteenth century and before. They were thought to compel interest, stimulate imagination, strengthen memory, and discourage trivial and selfish thoughts. The statue—particularly of the human body—had the effect of commanding one's attention and perhaps, if it was a good copy of a classical work, admiration. Nowadays, really wonderful pieces of garden statuary have become highly sought after and tend to fetch colossal prices—even those that are badly weathered and with pieces missing. In fact, the more weathered the better. But such pieces can also be difficult to integrate well into a modest garden, and mass-produced, scaled-down copies are considered as kitsch as garden gnomes. Consider, instead, other objects that will also give focus, create shape, or add a bit of tension: old chimney pots, architectural fragments, sundials, columns, urns, obelisks—even a fallen branch or an attractively shaped rock. Alternatively, there are plenty of sculptors, potters, and metalworkers making things that you might find suitable. Finally, don't forget the smaller things: think about wind chimes, mobiles, and, most environmentally friendly of all, houses for birds.

ROCKS

Rocks and stones in a garden represent millions of years of accumulated time. The Japanese used rocks as far back as the seventh century A.D.; some believed they symbolized the unchanging female, whereas plants were male. In both Japan and China, gardeners developed the art of the naturalistic landscape, with rivers, lakes, and bridges. Later on, small urban courtyards used one or two large, beautifully shaped rocks to symbolize a distant mountain. Consequently they became highly prized. Later still, rocks were also incorporated into aristocratic English gardens, as landscape gardeners built hillsides, waterfalls, and grottoes, in which hermits were supposed to live. Today, rocks are still as important to gardens, are just as expensive, and hold the same mythical qualities. It's about yin and yang. The use of hard and soft landscaping has been developed by garden designers to be as appropriate to a tiny garden or a roof terrace as to a huge country estate. Stone, from water-washed pebbles to jagged rocks and giant boulders, is readily available—some rocks are even predrilled to use as water features. But, more than most other garden elements, huge rocks are a challenge—not only to lift but also to visualize in situ.

WATER:
POOLS, FOUNTAINS & BRIDGES

Every garden needs water. Water has been an integral part of garden design since the ancient Egyptians, four thousand years ago. The Persians thought that no land beyond the sight of water could be considered a garden; their walled enclosures included streams and fountains that cooled the air and created what they called paradise. In Italy, during the Renaissance—utilizing the hilly locations of many of the palaces—some of the most imaginative garden plans were based on water being pumped to the top of a hill and allowing it to flow down again, passing through a multitude of ingenious spouts, jets, and rivulets. Grand country houses also had gardens that included natural looking ponds, lakes, rivers, and streams. In your own garden, the choices are simpler. If you don't have a spring, a well, or a local river to divert, try creating your own natural looking pond, stream, canal, brook, or waterfall using the various techniques that are available to you today. Water can be still, its reflective surface adding extra light to your garden; it can bubble over rocks, trickle from a spout, or spray in a multitude of fountain effects. With water, you will add perhaps the most relaxing, most magical quality of all: sound.

PERGOLAS, GAZEBOS & FOLLIES

Every country has its tradition of small garden structures—as a place to take tea or take in the view, play music, or write a great novel. A pavilion can provide shade in the summer or shelter from a storm, and the perfect focus for a garden party. It's a chance to set your architectural imagination free. A garden structure can be as simple as a poolside cabana, a rustic miniature English cottage, a sturdy Dutch gazebo, or a tranquil Japanese tea house. Such historic forms are inspiration for those who want a sylvan refuge in which to work, write, or entertain friends. Indeed, the garden structure is a building that brings you closer to nature. More practical are those garden structures that, while sometimes framing a view, serve primarily to support vines, roses, and other climbing plants. These are the arches, the pergolas, and the arbors, whose appeal lies not only in their appearance from a distance but in the experience of walking or sitting beneath them. Although a long pergola is suitable only for larger spaces, or to transform an awkward area along one side of a town house garden, an arch is ideal for creating a focal point, embracing a seat, or showcasing a spectacular flowering climber.

PARTERRES, HEDGES & TOPIARY

The art of pruning and trimming trees and bushes goes back to before the Romans, who practiced it to excess. It was revived again in the Middle Ages and was a craze in the seventeenth century and again in the nineteenth. Hedges—whether privet, yew, box, holly, oak, birch, or cypress—make an effective windbreak, a good background for plants, and a way of dividing a large garden into a variety of interesting and theatrical spaces. Really big hedges can take two or three hundred years to achieve and require ingenious ladder structures to maintain. In Japan, cutting and controlling the shape of trees and shrubs is an integral part of gardening, even in city squares and at traffic circles. In Bangkok and other parts of Thailand, topiary and its cousin bonsai adorn every temple and shrine. The French developed the art of the parterre, and the English devised their own take on topiary, as peacocks and small dogs in village cottage gardens contrast with massive compositions of imagination and caprice on grand estates. To start at the most modest level, you might try a specimen tree in the center of the lawn, or two rosemary bushes beside the front door. Whatever you choose, they will all require the same love of living sculpture and the same passion for pruning.

VISTAS

A vista provides a journey for the eye. It may not tell you the whole story, but it gives you a view of something in the distance—through a gap in a hedge, under an arch of climbing roses, down a narrow pathway, or beyond a door in a wall. The very first gardens, thousands of years ago, were walled enclosures. In the early fifteenth century, as Italian merchants began to build their villas outside the heat of the cities, they discovered that an opening in the wall of a garden provided an attractive view of the countryside. Soon, the walled enclosure was removed altogether, and the view—or partial view—became the thing. Depending on where you live, the view can reveal a church spire on a hilltop miles away, a pot on a stand, a piece of sculpture, or a tree across the road. Vistas are about hiding and revealing, sometimes obscuring a view in order to tempt you with only a glimpse of it at first. They are the "amuse-gueules" of gardening, the tasty morsel of which there may not be any more. Although a vista may be only a promise of something out of reach, by framing it and focusing on it, you are saying "This is also part of my garden, and my garden, by definition, is part of the wider world."

COLOR

Plants are, of course, the most exciting part of gardening—the only point, some might say. Planning a garden, putting in your plants or bulbs or cuttings—and watching them grow—goes to the heart of gardening; and there can be nothing more therapeutic, more gratifying, or more primal. Millions of people get tremendous pleasure from visiting gardens and garden centers, looking at flowers, and acquiring new varieties. In the late nineteenth century, the status of an English aristocrat was based on, among other things, the number of bedding plants—sometimes as many as fifty thousand—his gardeners planted. But there is another aspect of gardening that is much more difficult to get right, and that is composition. It is the skill of a great chef to decide what ingredients produce the most interesting flavors. So it is with gardening, and it's not only about color and soil and sun. Buy everything you like, stick it all in, and you'll get a hodgepodge of riotous joy. But be more selective, restrict your color palette, and think about the size and scale of the plants, the foliage color, and the leaf shapes, and you will be rewarded with a much more subtle result. Think of it as the difference between a brass-band concert and a violin concerto.

USEFUL
ADDRESSES

IN NORTH AMERICA

Aesthetica
P.O. Box 14
Gilbertsville, NY 13776
607-783-2114
www.rolandgreefkes.com
Garden ironwork, gates, and tables.

Aileen Minor American Antiques
30550 Washington St.
P.O. Box 40
Princess Anne, MD 21853
410-651-0075
www.aileenminor.com
Gallery specializing in antique fountains, statuary, benches, statues.

Amdega Machin Conservatories
P.O. Box 909
Front Royal, VA 22630
800-887-5648
www.amdega.comEnglish garden pavilions, summerhouses, and conservatories.

The Antique Rose Emporium
Route 5, Box 143
Brenham, TX 77833
800-441-0002
www
.antiqueroseemporium.com
Rustic cedar garden furniture.

Authentic Provence
522 Clematis St.
West Palm Beach,
FL 33401
561-805-9995
www.authenticprovence.com
French and English garden antiques, including urns, planters, spouts, fountains.

Baker's Lawn Ornaments
RD5, Box 265
Somerset, PA 15501
814-445-7028
www.bakerslawnorn.net
Gazing globes in seven colors.

The Bamboo Fencer
32 Germania St.
Jamaica Plain, MA 02130
617-524-6137
www.bamboofencer.com
Bamboo garden structures, birdhouses, bamboo poles.

Barbara Israel Garden Antiques
21 East 79th St.
New York, NY 10021
www.bi-gardenantiques.com
Antique garden ornament.

Bowbends
P.O. Box 900, Boston, MA 01740
508-779-6464
www.bowhouse.com/boxlock
Gazebos and other garden structures from arbors and pergolas to small bridges, trellage, and follies.

Brandon Industries, Inc.
1601 W. Wilmth Rd.
McKinney, TX 75069
800-247-1274
www.brandonindustries.com
Cast aluminum planters and urns.

Cape Cod Cupola
78 State Rd.
North Dartmouth, MA 02747
508-994-2119
www.capecodcupola.com
Weather vanes.

Christopher Filley Antiques
1721 W. 45th St.
Kansas City, MO 64111
816-561-1124
Old and antique fountains, statuary, urns.

Decorative Crafts, Inc.
50 Chestnut St.
P.O. Box 4308
Greenwich, CT 06830
203-531-1500
www.decorativecrafts.com
Assorted garden ornament, including Oriental porcelain garden seats.

Delaney & Cochran
156 South Park
San Francisco, CA 94107
415-896-2998
Fountains.

Design Toscano, Inc.
17 East Campbell St.
Arlington Heights, IL 60005
800-525-0733
www.designtoscano.com
Cast resin statues, figurines, birdbaths, gargoyles, plaques, and other ornament.

Devonshire English Garden Shop
1 East Washington St.
Middleburg, VA 20118
540-687-3623
New and antique garden ornament and furniture.

Doner Design
2175 Beaver Valley Pike
New Providence, PA 17560
717-786-8891
www.gardenartisans.com
Copper garden lights with useful website on one-of-a-kind garden art.

Dry Stone Walling Association
www.dswa.org.uk
See "Overseas" for a listing of certified and master dry stone wallers in the U.S. and Canada.

Fleur
10 Dakin Ave.
Mount Kisco, NY 10549
914-241-3400
www.fleur-newyork.com
Garden antiquary, statuary, topiaries, and decorative accessories.

Florentine Craftsmen, Inc.
46-24 28th St.
Long Island City, NY 11101
718-937-7632
www
.florentinecraftsmen.com
Handcrafted statuary, planters, urns, fountains.

Garden Accents
4 Union Hill Rd.
West Conshohocken,
PA 19428
800-296-5525
www.gardenaccents.com
Antique garden ornament, including urns, planters, stuatues, fountains.

Garden Escape
www.garden.com
Garden ornament through the Web.

Garden Magic
1930 Wake Forest Rd.
Raleigh, NC 27608
919-821-1997
www.gardenmagicstore.com
Light fixtures, trellises, topiary frames, trugs, and sundials.

Garden Park Antiques
7121 Cockrill Bend Blvd.
Nashville, TN 37209
615-254-1996
www.gardenpark.com
Garden and architectural antiques.

The Gardener
1836 Fourth St.
Berkeley, CA 94710
510-548-4545
www.thegardener.com
Assorted garden ornament and furniture.

Gardener's Supply Company
128 Intervale Rd.
Burlington, VT 05401
800-863-1700
www.gardeners.com
Assorted garden ornament.

Garth's Auction, Inc.
2690 Stratford Rd.
P.O. Box 369
Delaware, OH 43015
614-362-4771
www.garths.com
Auction house.

Good Directions
24 Ardmore Rd.
Stamford, CT 06902
800-346-7678
www.gooddirections.com
Copper and brass weather vanes.

GRDN
103 Hoyt St.
Brooklyn, NY 11217
718-797-3628
www.grdnbklyn.com
Garden ornament for the urban gardener.

Griggs Nursery
1021 David Ave.
Pacific Grove, CA 93950
408-373-4495
Garden ornament and large selection of terra-cotta pots. Also has a location in Carmel Valley, CA.

The Grove Homescapes
472 Lighthouse Ave.
Pacific Grove, CA 93950
408-656-0864
Giant iron sunflowers and other garden ornament.

The International Bonsai Arboretum
P.O. Box 23894
Rochester, NY 14692
585-334-2595
www.internationalbonsai.com
Bonsai containers and trays.

Jackson & Perkins
P.O. Box 1028
Medford, OR 97501
800-292-4769
www.jacksonandperkins.com
Trellises and arbors.

Kenneth Lynch & Sons, Inc.
84 Danbury Rd.
Wilton, CT 06897
203-762-8363
www.klynchandsons.com
Huge selection of garden ornament, from the diminutive to the monumental.

Kinsman Garden Company
Point Pleasure, PA 18950
800-733-4146
www.kinsmangarden.com
Assorted ornament, trellises, edgings, labels, pots. River Rd.

Lazy Hill Farm Designs
P.O. Box 235
Colerain, NC 27924
919-356-2828
www.lazyhill.com
Copper sculptures, hand-crafted birdhouses and feeders.

Linda Pearce Antiques
1214 West 47th St.
Kansas City, MO 64112
816-531-6255
www.lindawpearce.com
Old and antique fountains, statuary, architectural items, urns, planters.

Marcia Donahue
3017 Wheeler St.
Berkeley, CA 94705
510-540-8544
Stone garden sculptures.

The Marston House
Main Street
P.O. Box 517
Wiscasset, ME 04578
207-882-6010
www.marstonhouse.com
Antique English and New England garden ornament.

Marston Luce
1314 21st St. NW
Washington, DC 20036
202-775-9469
Old and antique garden furniture, urns, fountains, statuary.

Milaeger's Gardens
4838 Douglas Ave.
Racine, WI 53402
800-669-9956
www
.milaegers.emerchantpro.com
Gazing globes and assorted garden ornament.

Miss Trawick's Garden Shop
664 Lighthouse Ave.
Pacific Grove, CA 93950
408-375-4605
www.misstrawicks.com
Rustic trellises, garden furniture, and assorted ornament.

Museum Gift Shop and New England Bookstore
Old Sturbridge Village
1 Old Sturbridge Village Rd.
Sturbridge, MA 01566
Covered ridge bird feeder kit, country barn birdhouse kit, glazed redware flowerpots (replica of 1830s design).

N. P. Trent Antiques
3729 South Dixie Hwy.
West Palm Beach, FL 33405
561-832-0919
www.nptrentantiques.com
Period pieces only.

New England Garden Ornaments
38 E. Brookfield Rd.
North Brookfield, MA 01535
508-867-4474
www
.negardenornaments.com
Importers of UK garden ornament, including lead statues, fountains, planters, and rose arches.

Nichols Brothers Stoneworks
20209 Broadway
Snohomish, WA 98290
360-668-5434
www.nicholsbros.com
Dry-cast sandstone urns, pots, and small statues.

Olde Good Things
400 Gilligan St.
Scranton, PA 18508
888-233-9678
www.ogtstore.com
Specialists in architectural salvage with stores nationwide.

Robinson Iron
P.O. Box 1235
Robinson Rd.
Alexander City, AL 35010
205-329-8486
www.robinsoniron.com
Cast-iron garden ornament and reproduction fountains.

Romancing the Woods, Inc.
33 Raycliffe Dr.
Woodstock, NY 12498
845-246-1020
www.rtw-inc.com
Exterior rustic garden structures constructed of eastern red cedar in the tradition of 19th-century English gardens, and the Adirondack mountain camps.

Smith & Hawken
800 Redwood Hwy.
Mill Valley, CA 94941
415-381-1800
www.smithandhawken.com
Assorted garden ornament, furniture, planters, trellises, arbor lanterns, birdhouses. Also in retail stores nationwide.

Stone Forest
P.O. Box 2840
Santa Fe, NM 87504
505-986-8883
www.stoneforest.com
Hand-carved granite spheres, fountains, bowls, basins, lanterns, and benches.

Succulent Gardens & Gifts
3672 The Barnyard
Carmel, CA
831-624-0426
www.succulentgardens.com
Large assortment of wind chimes, stepping-stones, bonsai pots, and other ornament.

Tancredi & Morgen
7174 Carmel Valley Rd.
Carmel, CA 93923
831-625-4477
Antique garden ornament and old English pots.

Treillage, Ltd.
418 East 75th St.
New York, NY 10021
212-535-2288
www.treillageonline.com
Antique garden ornament.

Urban Archeology
143 Franklin St.
New York, NY 10013
212-431-4646
www.urbanarchaeology.com
High-end salvage and restoration, from cast-iron mermaid statues to poured stone Grecian urns.

Vintage Woodworks
Hwy. 34 S, P.O. Box 39
Quinlan, TX 75474
903-356-2158
www.vintagewoodworks.com
Garden gazebos.

Vixen Hill
69 E. Main St.
Elverson, PA 19520
800-423-2766
www.vixenhill.com
Garden gazebos and accessories.

Useful Addresses

Whitehall at the Villa Antiques
1213 East Franklin St.
Chapel Hill, NC 27514
919-942-3179
www.whitehallantiques.com
Antique fountains, statuary, and benches.

Wind & Weather
The Alvion St. Water Tower
P.O. Box 2320
Mendocino, CA 95460
800-922-9463
www.windandweather.com
Vertical and horizontal sundials, armillary-sphere sundials, gazing globes, and weather vanes.

Winterthur Museum & Garden
100 Enterprises Place
Dover, DE 19901
800-767-0500
www.winterthur.org
Iron garden furniture, brass cranes, birdhouses.

IN EUROPE

Adirondack Outdoors
www.adirondack.co.uk
Manufacturer of high quality outdoor furniture, primarily in the Adirondack style, built using naturally durable materials and with emphasis on comfort and style.
Page 99, row 3, no. 1

African Thatch Company, Ltd.
www
.africanthatchcompany.co.uk
African-style gazebos made from wooden poles and South African cape reed thatch tiles.

Agriframes
www.agriframes.co.uk
Metal arches, obelisks, gazebos, pergolas, and screens.

Apta
www.apta.co.uk
Supplies a comprehensive range of pots to garden centers, ranging from metal, terra-cotta to various ceramic finishes.

Barlow Tyrie, Ltd.
www.teak.com
Seats, benches, and garden furniture in teak.

Bellamont Topiary
www.bellamont-topiary.co.uk
Largest collection of field-grown box topiary and hedging in the UK. Plants sold by shape (sphere, cone, cube, spiral, egg, onion, pyramid, fondant) and size.

Benchmark Furniture
www
.benchmark-furniture.com
Excellence in design, materials and craftsmanship, producing contemporary classics that will last a lifetime. Designed by well-known names including the Azumis, Terence Conran, Thomas Heatherwick and Russell Pinch.
Page 86, bottom left
Page 97, bottom left

Bradstone
www.bradstone.com
Paving, "log" sleepers, decorative aggregrates (cobbles, stones, rocks), edging, and walling.

Augustus Brandt Antiques
www.augustus-brandt-antiques.co.uk
Antique garden furniture and pots.

The Brooke Pottery
www.thebrookepottery.com
Collection of large English urns, classically designed with a contemporary edge. All urns are handmade from high-firing English terra-cotta clay using traditional skills of hand-throwing, coiling, and press molding.

Bulbeck Foundry
www.bulbeckfoundry.co.uk
English lead statuary, urns, cisterns, and pots.

Cannock Gates
www.cannockgates.co.uk
Large selection of gates.

Capital Garden Products, Ltd.
www.capital-garden.com
Decorative plant containers and architectural features. Also custom-made solutions tailored to clients' needs. Worldwide delivery.
Opposite page 1
Page 63, row 3, no.1
Page 71, row 4, no.2

Page 75, row 2, no. 1
Page 97, row 3, no.1

Chairworks, Ltd.
www.chairworks.info
Plant climbers, covers, arbors, gazebos, benches, edgings, and fence panels (hurdles) made of hazel or willow.
Page 31, row 3, no.2
Page 88, bottom left

Chilstone
www.chilstone.com
Traditional style garden ornaments, pots, urns, troughs, plinths, fountains, birdbaths, dovecotes, statues, and sculpture.
Page 71, row 2, no.3
Page 114, centre bottom

John Close Sundials
www.johnclosesundials.co.uk
Large range of quality made sundials, armillary sundials, wall dials, and horizontal sun dials.

Connoisseur Sundials
www.sun-dials.net
Accurate sundials and armillary spheres. Handmade in brass and bronze.

Coulson's Bridges
www.coulsonsbridges.co.uk
Elegant curved bridges individually crafted to any design.

Andrew Crace
www.andrewcrace.co.uk
Garden seats, benches, tables, sun-loungers, tree-seats, and planters. Handmade in iroko or oak.
Page 82, row 1, no.2
Page 82, row 2, no.1 & 2
Page 82, row 3, no.1 & 2
Page 83, top left
Page 84, row 2, no.2 & 3
Page 84, row 3, no.2
Page 85, row 4, no.2
Page 86, row 1, no.1 & 2
Page 86, row 2, no.1
Page 86, row 3, no.1 & 2
Page 99, bottom right

Cranborne Stone
www.cranbornestone.co.uk
Balustrading, finials, coping stones, urns, planters in hand-cast, reconstituted stone. Standard and custom-made designs.

Creta Cotta
www.cretacotta.co.uk
Handmade frost-proof Cretan terra-cotta pots.

The Cutting Edge Collection
www.cutting-edge.gb.com
Arbors, gazebos, and summerhouses. Also a few bronze, resin bronze, or lead water features and ornaments.

Cyan
www
.cyan-teak-furniture.com
Benches, garden furniture, tubs, and plants.

Design and Landscape
www
.designandlandscape.co.uk
Contemporary sculpture, water features, furniture, pots, and planters.

Dorset Reclamation
www
.dorsetreclamation.co.uk
Decorative architectural and garden antiques, including flagstones, paving bricks, quarry tiles, stone troughs, birdbaths, benches, statues, staddle stones, and gates.

Gary Drostle
www.drostle.com
www.mosaicmakers.co.uk
Mosaic artist with useful website on how to commission a mosaic.

Eden Furniture, Ltd.
www.teak-furniture.co.uk
Garden furniture, benches, and sun-loungers.

English Garden Carpentry Co., Ltd.
www.egcc.biz
Arbors, bridges, gazebos, pavilions, pergolas, fencing, gates, and custom-made garden structures.

English Hurdle
www.hurdle.co.uk
Hurdles but also gates, arches, arbors using willow and similar materials.

Field Farm Enterprises Ltd
www.cedarshed.co.uk
Lots of different sizes and shapes of gazebos in solid cedar.

Forest
www.forestgarden.co.uk
The UK's largest manufacturer of wooden fences, arches, arbors, pergolas, trellises, and planters.

Robert Foster
www
.sundialsbyrobertfoster.co.uk
Handmade sundials and armillary spheres.

French Stone (UK), Ltd.
www.frenchstone.co.uk
French stone fountains, benches, urns, statues, and ornaments made from cast stone, sculpted stone, or terra-cotta.

Garden Iron
www.gardeniron.co.uk
Wrought-iron garden structures, folding furniture and plant supports.

Gardening Thoughts, Ltd.
www
.gardeningthoughts.co.uk
Tree seats, arbors, arches, bridges, summerhouses, and log cabins.

Garpa
www.garpa.co.uk
Furniture and accessories for discerning taste—timeless, elegant, and weatherproof.

Gaze Burville Ltd
www.gazeburville.com
Fine outdoor furniture.
Page 82, row 4, no.2
Page 85, row 5, no.2

Global Gardens, Ltd.
www.global-gardens.co.uk
Fine handmade Italian frost-resistant pots, planters, and urns.

Gloster Furniture, Ltd.
www.gloster.com
From traditional to contemporary, products to suit all requirements and locations. Benches, tables, armchairs, sun-loungers, and occasional furniture.
Page 82, top left
Page 99, bottom left

Grange Fencing, Ltd.
www.grangefen.co.uk

Arbors, gazebos, arches, pergolas, gates, and garden fencing.
Page 31, row 5, no.1, 2 & 3
Page 31, row 3, no.3
Page 99, bottom left

H. Crowther, Ltd.
www.hcrowther.co.uk
Large selection of antique garden ornaments.

Haddonstone, Ltd.
www.haddonstone.com
Pots, urns, troughs, plinths, pool and fountain accessories, statuary, birdbaths, sundials, garden furniture, and lawn edgings.

David Harber, Ltd.
www.davidharber.com
Water features, sculptures, and sundials. Plinths in a range of styles.

Christopher Hartnoll
www
.christopherhartnoll.co.uk
Iron garden furniture.
Page 41, row 3, no.1

Heal's
www.heals.co.uk
Seasonal collections of stylish outdoor furniture and accessories.

Hillhout, Ltd.
www.hillhout.nl
Manufacturer of sturdy wooden garden products, such as fencing, pergolas, edgings, furniture, planters, and gazebos.

Hopes Grove Nurseries
www
.hopesgrovenurseries.co.uk
Extensive lists of all types of hedging plants and box and yew topiary.

IOTA Garden and Home, Ltd.
www.iotagarden.com
Contemporary planters (granite, fibreglass, slate, and terrazzo). Granite water features and mirror polished steel art.

The Iron Made Company
www.ironmade.co.uk
Specialize in folding and easy-to-assemble ironware furniture for the home and garden.

Useful Addresses

Italian Terrace
www.italianterrace.co.uk
A collection of urns, vases and plaques handmade by craftsmen in Italy. Each piece, either classical or contemporary, has a wonderful aged and weathered texture.

Jacksons
www.jacksons-fencing.co.uk
Timber fencing, balustrades, gates, trellises, pergolas, and planters. Also farm gates, post and rail fencing, chain mesh, cleft chestnut, and centry bar fencing.

Jade Pavilions
www.jade-pavilions.com
Tea-houses, temples, pavilions, bridges, and entrances. Standard or custom designs.

JapanGarden.co.uk
www.japangarden.co.uk
Internet-based business supplying all types of items for Japanese gardens: bamboo screens, water features including deer scarers, rocks, gazebos, bridges, etc.

Juro Antiques
www.juro.co.uk
Wide assortment of garden antiques, including stone troughs, cidermills, staddle stones, statuary, fountains, and garden furniture.

Kent Balusters
www.kentbalusters.co.uk
Balustrades, columns, pergolas, temples, ball finials, steps, and paving.

The Landscape Ornament Company, Ltd.
www .landscapeornament.com
Timeless designs from the celebrated English landscape architect Michael Balston together with contemporary artists and sculptors. An inspired range of timber furniture, stone ornaments, and earthenware pots.
Page 84, row 3, no.1
Page 84, row 4, no.2
Page 84, row 5, no.1 & 2
Page 97, row 2, no.1

Chris Lewis
www.studiopottery.co.uk
Large and small garden pots, garden seats and sculptural pieces—all 100% frost-proof. Also individual pieces and special commissions.
Page 64, center bottom
Page 96, row 2, no.2
Page 142, row 4, no.3

Magma Designs
www.magmadesigns.co.uk
(+44) 0207 2288 466
Wide range of pots, urns, troughs and "riverstone" cobbled stone patterns mounted on mesh—for floor or wall covering, suitable for indoor and outdoor.
Endpapers
Page 39 top right

Marshalls
www.marshalls.co.uk
Paths, edging, walls, decorative aggregates (pebbles, cobbles, glass).

Marston and Langinger, Ltd.
www .marston-and-langinger.com
Selection of furniture in wire for garden and conservatory.

Metallicus, Ltd.
www.metallicus.co.uk
Designs and builds contemporary metalwork including: furniture, tree seats, water features, and planters.

Chris Nangle Furniture Design
www .chrisnanglefurniture.co.uk
Landscape furniture designed and made from prime grade English oak and marine stainless steel. All timber is from well-managed English woodlands.
Page 84, row 2, no.1
Page 102, row 3, no.2

Natural Driftwood Sculptures
www .driftwoodsculptures.co.uk
Originating from the lakes of Canada, the Western Red Cedar driftwood sculptures have a unique silver coloring, which complements their wonderful shapes. Mail order.

New Dawn Furniture
www.newdawnfurniture.co.uk
Custom-made garden furniture in oak or teak.

Norton Garden Structures
www .nortongardenstructures.co.uk
Gazebos, summerhouses, arbors, bridges, pergolas, and garden art.

Oak Tree Pottery
www.oaktreepottery.co.uk
Original ceramic garden sculptures made to order in the studio.

Oakleaf Gates
www.oakleafgates.co.uk
Design and produce custom-made gates to the very highest standards of craftsmanship. Constructed using seasoned oak.

Original Features
www.originalfeatures.co.uk
Supplies products for restoring Olde English tiles such as black-and-white tiled paths.

Outer Eden Trading
www.outer-eden.co.uk
Outdoor furniture with an emphasis on build, quality, and style.

Oxford Planters, Ltd.
www.oxfordplanters.co.uk
Topiary (mostly box, yew, and bay) in various shapes, plus a good range of containers (wooden from Belgium, galvanised metal from Paris, and lead planters from Oxford).

Oxley's Furniture CO., Ltd.
www.oxleys.com
Handmade fine quality cast aluminum furniture, which is rust-proof, rot-proof, and will withstand the effects of sun, wind, and rain.

Plantstuff, Ltd.
www.plantstuff.com
Small birdhouses, feeders, and nesting boxes. Butterfly, ladybird and hedgehog houses. Mail order.

Pots and Pithoi
www.potsandpithoi.com
Painted teak garden furniture, plus claims to have the world's largest selection of Cretan pots.

Quercus UK, Ltd.
sales@quercusfencing.co.uk
Stylish oak fencing panels that allow air to pass through.

Room In the Garden
www.roominthegarden.com
Elegant rusted iron arches, gazebos, and pavilions.

Sitting Spiritually
www.sittingspiritually.co.uk
Martin Young is a highly respected creator of handmade swing seats and garden chairs.
Page 95, row 2, no.1

Sleeper Supplies, Ltd.
www.sleeper-supplies.co.uk
Specializes in the supply of new and used railway sleepers, crossing timbers, and telegraph poles.

Specialist Aggregates, Ltd.
www .specialistaggregates.com
Chippings, gravel, cobbles, pebbles, rocks, and slate by 1 ton or half ton load.

Jonathan Stockton
www .johnathanstockton.co.uk
Designer and maker of contemporary chic outdoor furniture. The quality of design, materials, and craftsmanship mean that the pieces can be left outdoors all year round and are equally well suited for yachts, pools, and ski chalets as well as gardens.
Page 101

Stonemarket, Ltd.
www.stonemarket.co.uk
Paving, walling, brick, granite, decorative aggregates (pebbles, cobbles, boulders, slate).

Sunny Aspects, Ltd.
info@sunnyaspects.com
Frosted translucent polypropylene fence panels for patios, windows in boundary fencing, and walltops. Resistant to U.V. rays and low temperatures.

Teak and Garden BU
www.teak-garden.nl
Comprehensive range of garden furniture, bronze urns, tubs, and statuary.

Tendercare
www.tendercare.co.uk
A source of mature specimens of hardy plants beloved of top garden designers, has a section devoted to large scale topiary plants of all types.

Terrace and Garden, Ltd.
www.terraceandgarden.com
Garden benches for indoor, conservatory or occasional outdoor use.
Page 90, row 2, no.2

Time Circles
www.timecircles.co.uk
Unusual stones and sculpture, including holed stones, megaliths and symbol stones. Thirty to forty pieces on show.

The UK Gate Company
www.theukgatecompany.com
Choose from a range of existing styles or have one built from your own design from a choice of timbers or iron. With an optional automation system.

The Victorian Gate and Seating Company
www.gardenseats.com
Traditional style iron garden seats, chairs, and gates. Appointment only.

Walcot Reclamation
www.walcot.com
Staddle stones, birdbaths, millstones, urns, troughs, sundials, and pots.

Sarah Walton
www.sarahwalton.co.uk
Sarah Walton produces five shapes of birdbath. All stand on green oak bases the height of which can be specified by the customer. Also produces saltglazed tiles.
Page 143

Whichford Pottery
www.whichfordpottery.com
Using throwing and pressing techniques passed down over centuries, the highly skilled potters at Whichford Pottery are dedicated to making only the finest terra-cotta flowerpots. All Whichford flowerpots carry a 10-year frost-proof guarantee and can be left outside all year round.

Wilstone
www.wilstone.com
Specialists in original hand-carved stone, wrought-iron and unique, custom-made architectural pieces to landscape designers, architects, and gardening enthusiasts.
Page 70, row 2, no.3
Page 71, row 3, no.3 & 4
Page 71, row 4, no.1
Page 100, top left
Page 106, bottom right
Page 108, top centre
Page 112, top left
Page 116, row 5, no.2
Page 151, row 3, no.2

D.W. Windsor
www.dwwindsor.co.uk
Over 30 designs of contemporary style seats and benches.

Woodlodge Products Ltd
www.woodlodge.co.uk
Major distributor of plant containers from the Far East to UK garden centers.

Acknowledgments

Well, did you count them?

How could you? I have no clue as to precisely how many ideas there are here—most of the pictures have a multitude in each. They are the work of many thousands of gardeners, builders, craftsmen, and homeowners over many years. Thanks to their enthusiasm, care, attention, passion, and ingenuity, we can be encouraged to try a bit harder in our search for a more original solution, so that we, too, can inspire others. My thanks to all those who have opened their gardens to my eclectic eye—and to all of us. That's the thing about gardeners: their generosity. Most great gardens, wherever they are, are full of ideas just waiting to be enjoyed, adopted, and reapplied. In fact, you might say that's what gardening is all about—putting your own interpretation on the standard formula. Except that nothing is standard. Just looking around, you can see that things are being reinvented all the time—new products, new concepts, new technology. Garden designers are some of the most creative people, and their task is perhaps the most difficult, because they're dealing with elements that are so unpredictable and with ingredients (plants) that never stay the same from one week to the next, one year to the next. Perhaps that's why gardening is so exciting, so frustrating, so rewarding.

My sincere thanks to all those who have helped with this book in other ways, too. Neighbors, friends, and family whose gardens I've included or who have taken me to see some amazing gardens over the years: Suzanne Slesin, Sherri Donghia, Terence Conran, Stan Lovenworth, Sam Tallerico, Norman Camm, Drew Cliff, Darren Rees, Brian Thompson, Hardy Jones, Susan Scrymgour, and Gladys Cliff. Thanks, too, to the manufacturers and craftsmen who sent me pictures of their products. In particular: Lee Galea, Richard Player, Andrew Crace, Jonathan Stockton, John McMillan, Sarah Walton, Chris Lewis, Chris Nangle, Martin Young, and Rosemary Case.

In Britain, The National Gardens Scheme is a tremendous organization that allows us to see hundreds of small private gardens. By contrast, the National Trust plays an important role in restoring, promoting, and maintaining gardens all over the country, and the Royal Horticultural Society is the U.K.'s leading gardening charity, dedicated to advancing horticulture and promoting good gardening through their annual and monthly shows and their own gardens at Wisley, Rosemoor, Harlow Carr, and Hyde Hall. For more information, log on to www.rhs.org.uk.

For their enthusiastic hands-on help in the production of this book I must thank the devoted commitment of Jane O'Shea, Katherine Case, Samantha Rolfe, and Laura Herring, the production team at Quadrille, led by Vincent Smith and Bridget Fish, and the continued help and support of John Scott.

Page 4 © Corinne Korda/Redcover.com
Pages 6–7 © Andrew Lawson
Page 8 © Fritz von der Schulenburg—The Interior Archive/designer: John Stefanidis
Page 11 © Andrew Lawson/designer: Christopher Bradley-Hole, R.H.S. Chelsea 2005
Page 87 Garden Picture Library/Mark Bolton
Page 97 Andrew Lawson/The Garden Collection
Page 115 Frieder Blickle/Bilderberg
Page 119 Liz Eddison/The Garden Collection: Prieuré Notre-Dame d'Orsan, France
Pages 124–5 © Elizabeth Whiting & Associates/Alamy
Page 129 © Jerry Harpur/design: Ursel Gut for The Schneider Garden
Page 134 GAP Photos/John Glover, row 3, no.2
Page 133 © Andrew Lawson/Private Garden, Quebec
Page 161 GAP Photos / Mark Bolton, The Abbey House Gardens
Page 165 © Ed Wheeler/CORBIS, Gardens of Quinta da Bacalhoa, Portugal
Page 174 Nicola Stocken Tomkins/The Garden Collection: Wayford Manor

Editorial Director Jane O'Shea
Art Director Helen Lewis
Designer/Photographer Stafford Cliff
Picture Research Samantha Rolfe
Design Assistant Katherine Case
Editor Laura Herring
Production Vincent Smith, Bridget Fish

First published in 2007 by
Quadrille Publishing Limited
Alhambra House
27–31 Charing Cross Road
London WC2H 0LS
www.quadrille.co.uk

Published in the United States in 2008
by Artisan
A Division of Workman Publishing
Company, Inc.
225 Varick Street
New York, NY 10014-4381
www.artisanbooks.com

Design and layout copyright © 2007
Quadrille Publishing Limited
Text copyright © 2007 Stafford Cliff

All rights reserved. No portion of this
book may be reproduced—mechanically,
electronically, or by any other means,
including photocopying—without written
permission of the publisher.

Library of Congress Control Number:
2007925974

ISBN-13: 978-1-57965-348-4

Printed in China
First American printing, January 2008

10 9 8 7 6 5 4 3 2 1